CRAZY DIAMONDS

Copyright © 2025 HEADLINE PUBLISHING GROUP Limited

The right of Malcolm Croft to be identified as the Author of the Work has been asserted by him in accordance with the Copyright, Designs and Patents Act 1988.

First published in 2025 by OH
An Imprint of HEADLINE PUBLISHING GROUP LIMITED

1

Disclaimer:

All trademarks, copyright, quotations, company names, registered names, products, characters, logos and catchphrases used or cited in this book are the property of their respective owners. This book has not been licensed, approved, sponsored, or endorsed by Pink Floyd.

Apart from any use permitted under UK copyright law, this publication may only be reproduced, stored, or transmitted, in any form, or by any means, with prior permission in writing of the publishers or, in the case of reprographic production, in accordance with the terms of licences issued by the Copyright Licensing Agency.

Cataloguing in Publication Data is available from the British Library

ISBN 978-1-80069-635-8

Compiled and written by: Malcolm Croft
Editorial: Saneaah Muhammad
Designed and typeset in Avenir by: Andy Jones
Project manager: Russell Porter
Production: Rachel Burgess
Printed and bound in China

Headline's policy is to use papers that are natural, renewable and recyclable products and made from wood grown in well-managed forests and other controlled sources. The logging and manufacturing processes are expected to conform to the environmental regulations of the country of origin.

HEADLINE PUBLISHING GROUP LIMITED
An Hachette UK Company
Carmelite House, 50 Victoria Embankment, London EC4Y 0DZ

The authorised representative in the EEA is Hachette Ireland, 8 Castlecourt Centre, Castleknock Road, Castleknock, Dublin 15, D15 YF6A, Ireland

www.headline.co.uk   www.hachette.co.uk

CRAZY DIAMONDS

THE LITTLE GUIDE TO PINK FLOYD
UNOFFICIAL AND UNAUTHORIZED

CONTENTS

INTRODUCTION — 6

8
CHAPTER
ONE

INTERSTELLAR
UNDERGROUND

40
CHAPTER
TWO

QUADRAPHONIC
PSYCHADELICS

76
CHAPTER
THREE

HIGH
HOPES

104

CHAPTER
FOUR

LUNAR LUNACY

136

CHAPTER
FIVE

MIND CONTROL

174

CHAPTER
SIX

COMFORTABLY FAMOUS

INTRODUCTION

Pink Floyd need no introduction. They are, without a doubt, the most famous interstellar rock group ever to escape the London underground – the city's psychedelic scene of the late 1960s – and to bocame so stratospherically significant that their music is now embedded into every atom of popular culture since their 1973 conceptual masterpiece, *The Dark Side of the Moon*. That album, of course, rocketed them from being highly respected radio heroes to the objects of adoration by prog rock fans worldwide, a genre that Pink Floyd transcended above all others.

In the pre-digital age, this mind-bending band of quadraphonic thrill seekers ruled the FM-airwaves and set the standards for stadium rock by revolutionizing light, sound and stage shows – the technological marvel of which still dazzles our eyes and rings in our ears today.

It hasn't been an easy journey, of course. Nothing in rock and roll ever is. Pink Floyd's path to selling more than 250 million records has, inevitably, been rocked by ferocious inner-band tension with division bells being repeatedly rung between members Syd Barrett, Roger Waters, David Gilmour, Rick Wright and Nick Mason. From founding songwriter Barrett's decline due to LSD misuse in 1967 to Waters' and Gilmour's bitter legal disputes over the band name in the 1980s, Pink Floyd's foundation of peace and love went out the window sometime around 1974, if not earlier.

Thankfully, even if the band members no longer speak to each other, their music still speaks for itself, a light that still shines on like a crazy diamond in the sky, untouchable but unbreakable.

This *Little Guide to Pink Floyd* is the pocket-sized celebration every Floyd fan deserves, a tiny tome that speaks the truth of the band's unstoppable rise to fame, in the words of those who made it happen. Enjoy!

CHAPTER
ONE

INTERSTELLAR UNDERGROUND

Pink Floyd's origins were rooted in London's psychedelic and hippy underground scene, a community that embraced the band's wild and trippy flights into unstructured musical madness.

With singer-songwriter Syd Barrett piloting the spaceship, the group released two groundbreaking albums.

However, just as they were about to takeoff, their main engine turned on, tuned in and dropped out…

INTESTELLAR UNDERGROUND

All we can do is make records which we like. If the kids don't, then they won't buy it.

Syd Barrett, on making music the kids will like, *Melody Maker*, 9 December 1967

No reason. It just sounds like a nice name to us. It's really just a registration mark. It's better than calling ourselves CCE338, or something like that.

Roger Waters, on the reason behind why the band are called Pink Floyd, *Tonarskvall 3 Radio*, 10 September 1967

INTESTELLAR UNDERGROUND

I clearly remember sitting with Syd making a drawing of all the equipment we thought we'd ever need, which consisted of two Vox AC30s. Later, we formed various bands and gradually became 'The Pink Floyd Sound'.

Roger Waters, on his early musical alliances with Syd, *MOJO*, March 2003

The Evolution of Pink Floyd's Name

From **1963** to **1967**

1. **Sigma 6**
2. **Meggadeaths**
3. **The Abdabs**
4. **The Screaming Abdabs**
5. **Leonard's Lodgers**
6. **The Spectrum Five**
7. **The Tea Seat**
8. **The Pink Floyd Sound**
9. **The Pink Floyd**
10. **Pink Floyd**

Syd Barrett came up with the name "Pink Floyd" by merging the names of his two favourite American blues guitarists: Pink Anderson and Floyd Counsel.

You can't take four people of this mental level – architects, an artist and even an educational cyberneticist – give them big success and not expect them to get confused. But they are coming through a sort of de-confusing period now. They are not just a record group.

PINK FLOYD

They really pull people in to see them and their album has been terrifically received in this country and America. I think they've got tremendous things ahead of them. They are really only just starting.

"

Co-manager **Peter Jenner**, on the band's formative rise to success with Syd as leader, with their debut album *The Piper at the Gates of Dawn*, *Melody Maker*, 9 December 1967

INTESTELLAR UNDERGROUND

I don't know that there was really much conflict, except that perhaps the way we started to play wasn't as impressive as it might've been. I mean, it was done very well, rather than considerably exciting. One thinks of it all as a dream.

Syd Barrett, on the earliest rehearsals of Pink Floyd, *Melody Maker*, 27 March 1971

PINK FLOYD

We've had problems with our equipment and we can't get the P.A. to work because we play extremely loudly. It's a pity because Syd writes great lyrics and nobody ever hears them.

Roger Waters, on the band's difficulty finding equipment that could handle their sound in their early days, *Melody Maker*, 5 August 1967

INTESTELLAR UNDERGROUND

Syd and I met at a Saturday morning art class in Homerton College in Cambridge when I was eight and Syd was six. My mother knew his parents, but we didn't get pally right away. Then he came to the same grammar school as me and when rock started, when I was about 14, we started playing guitars together.

Roger Waters, on his early friendship with Syd, *MOJO*, March 2003

> I was living in Highgate with [Roger], we shared a place there, and got a van and spent a lot of our grant on pubs. We were playing Stones numbers…
> I picked up playing guitar quite quickly… I was soon playing on the professional scene and began to write from there.

Syd Barrett, on his earliest days as a musician and living in London with Roger, *Melody Maker*, 27 March 1971

INTESTELLAR UNDERGROUND

Pink Floyd's setlist from their legendary Queen Elizabeth Hall gig, May 12, 1967.

It was also the world's first-ever surround-sound concert and the band's debut performance of its custom-built quadraphonic speaker system.

1. **"Matilda Mother"**
2. **"Flaming"**
3. **"The Scarecrow"**
4. **"See Emily Play"**
5. **"Bike"**
6. **"Arnold Layne"**
7. **"Candy and a Currant Bun"**
8. **"Pow R. Toc H."**
9. **"Interstellar Overdrive"**
10. **"Lucifer Sam"**

During the gig, the band chopped wood on stage, a roadie in an admiral's costume threw daffodils into the crowd and a machine filled the hall with bubbles. The group were banned from ever playing there again.

We were all students together in the first year. I remember we played the songs for the publisher and he said [that Syd's] songs were quite good but 'forget the band'. I think if we'd listened to anyone who had any taste at the time we'd have all folded up right then and there. But fortunately, we were so egocentric and just carried on.

Nick Mason, on Syd's impressive song writing in the late 1960s, *The Source*, 1984

INTESTELLAR UNDERGROUND

It's a simple matter, really. Syd just had a big overdose of acid and that was it. It was very frightening, and I couldn't believe what had happened, because I remember we had to do a radio show, and we were waiting for him, and he didn't turn up. And then he came the next day, and he was a different person.

Roger Waters, on Syd's LSD misuse and disappearance, *The Source*, 1984

> Syd was a strange guy even back in Cambridge… His father's death affected him very heavily and his mother always pampered him – made him out to be a genius of sorts. I remember I really started to get worried when I went along to the session for 'See Emily Play'. He had that stare, y'know.

David Gilmour, on Syd's descent into LSD misuse and his strangeness, *NME*, 13 April 1974

INTESTELLAR UNDERGROUND

> When 'Emily' was a hit, we did *Top of the Pops*, and the third week we did it, Syd didn't want to know. He got down there in an incredible state and said he wasn't gonna do it. We finally discovered the reason was that John Lennon didn't have to do *Top of the Pops*, so he didn't.

Roger Waters, on Syd's increasingly erratic behaviour towards the end of his tenure within the group, *Melody Maker*, 27 March 1971

We didn't recognize what was going on [with Syd]… He became really quite psychotic – you know, attacking girlfriends. We should have recognized what was happening and gone our separate ways, but we didn't, because we thought we needed him, and we didn't know enough about what was going on.

Nick Mason, on Syd's psychotic breakdown due to his LSD usage, *Uncut*, 14 March 2017

INTESTELLAR UNDERGROUND

The space thing was a joke. None of those pieces were about outer space. They were about *inner* space. That's all it's ever been about – human beings and their insides.

Roger Waters, on Pink Floyd's early "interstellar space rock" sound, *Rolling Stone*, 19 November 1987

PINK FLOYD

In the summer of '68, there were groupies everywhere; they'd come and look after you like a personal maid, do your washing, sleep with you and then leave with a dose of the clap.

Rick Wright, on the group's groupies, Q magazine, November 1994

INTESTELLAR UNDERGROUND

We were very English, and I wouldn't dream of living anywhere other than England. The early Pink Floyd was quintessentially English. It wasn't your usual rock'n'roll, R&B stuff, which is very American-oriented.

99

David Gilmour, on Pink Floyd being English, *Interview* magazine, July 1994

When [Syd] was still in the band in the later stages, we got to the point where any one of us was likely to tear his throat out at any minute because he was so impossible.

Roger Waters, on Syd's withdrawal and strange behaviour during his final days in the group, *Melody Maker*, 27 March 1971

INTESTELLAR UNDERGROUND

[*Saucerful of Secrets*] was the end of Syd. When Syd left it wasn't
like Roger mounted to the bridge and shouted 'I am now the captain! You will obey!' Though now I think, why didn't he do that and just get it over with?

Nick Mason, on recording *A Saucerful of Secrets*, *Maxim* magazine, January 2002

> Initially, it got really embarassing. I had to say things like, 'Syd, I'm going out to get a pack of cigarettes' and then go off and play a gig. Of course, eventually, he worked out what was going on.

Rick Wright, on Syd's inability to function as a member of Pink Floyd, *Syd Barrett: A Very Irregular Head*, Rob Chapman, 2010 – the first definitive bioigraphy of Syd Barrett

INTESTELLAR UNDERGROUND

[Syd] was looking for enlightenment and also for that LSD enlightenment… I think he reacted badly to the drug. But I think he then kept doing it because of what he wanted to get from it. He kept doing it when he probably should have just said, 'This doesn't work for me.'

Nick Mason, on Syd's LSD usage, *Uncut*, 14 March 2017

Syd was a major talent as a songwriter... people who don't perhaps entirely achieve all their potential become even more legendary.

Nick Mason, on Syd's legacy and legend, *The Source*, 1984

INTESTELLAR UNDERGROUND

Syd was indeed without doubt the instigator of the first Floyd. At the beginning, he wrote almost all of the songs, he was the creative fulcrum of the group and The Pink Floyd to Syd meant 'interstellar rock music'.

But the public don't accept the change, and I think that *Dark Side* has proved that Pink Floyd aren't interstellar rock music and that they haven't been for years.

Nick Mason, on Pink Floyd's move away from space rock, *Ciao 2001* magazine, 25 May 1975

INTESTELLAR UNDERGROUND

Suddenly, we had a recording contract, so we were pretty full of ourselves. The most humbling part was that the Beatles were working on *Sgt. Pepper* at the same time, just down the hall. They were recording 'Lovely Rita'. It sounded so sophisticated. That was more alarming than any feeling of what was expected of us.

Nick Mason, on recording *The Piper at the Gates of Dawn*, *Maxim* magazine, January 2002

Syd was absolutely up for it… There was no suggestion at all that he might be uncomfortable with the idea of becoming a pop star.

Nick Mason, on Syd's desire for fame, despite considering himself an artist, *MOJO*, October 2007

INTESTELLAR UNDERGROUND

[Syd and I] both had similar interests – rock'n'roll, danger, sex and drugs, probably in that order.

Roger Waters, on his bond with Syd, *Musician* magazine, May 1992

> **Syd did enough for all of us.**

David Gilmour, on tripping and Syd's downfall following his destructive misuse of LSD, *Rolling Stone*, 13 October 2011

CHAPTER
TWO

QUADRAPHONIC PSYCHADELICS

In 1968, Syd Barrett's psychedelic trips got the better of his mental health and forced him to retreat from not just the band, but from life entirely. He was rarely ever seen outside again.

His replacement, David Gilmour, was a thrilling addition to the group and one that course-corrected the group's forward projectory. Suddenly, the band had found their feet, and their focus, and were once again looking up to the stars…

QUADRAPHONIC PSYCHADELICS

> I think we were all pretty pragmatic after Syd left. We were absolutely all determined to not have to go back to work. Not to have to get a proper job. And in order not to have to get a proper job, you have to work at it. You have to do whatever you need to do to keep it going.

Roger Waters, on Syd's departure from the group and continuing to move forward with the band, *Rolling Stone*, 13 October 2011

He's a wonderful singer and a great guitar player. What more could you want? And he's also a nice bloke. Good fun, likes a laugh and all that. It wasn't like, 'Oh, he's a great guitar player and a beautiful singer, but he's weird.'

Roger Waters, on David Gilmour joining the band in 1968, *Rolling Stone*, 13 October 2011

QUADRAPHONIC PSYCHADELICS

> **"** Nice white English architecture students getting funky is a bit of an odd thought. **"**

David Gilmour, on dropping funkier songs, such as Booker T's "Green Onions" from their early live sets, *Rolling Stone*, 17 March 2003

20 January 1968

The date of the last gig Pink Floyd performed with Syd Barrett – an end-of-the-pier show at Hastings Pier, Hastings. Those that were there claimed that a "clearly high" Syd had to be held back from jumping off the pier, believing he could fly with the seagulls.

> "I don't really remember the gig. I know we did it; there were only two or three of those combined five-piece things. But Hastings Pier wouldn't have been our finest moment."

Nick Mason commenting on the last Pink Floyd gig with Syd Barrett, *Uncut*, 14 March 2017

QUADRAPHONIC PSYCHADELICS

That was always my big fight in Pink Floyd. To try and drag it kicking and screaming back from the borders of space, from the whimsy that Syd was into, to my concerns, which were much more political and philosophical.

Roger Waters, on the difference between his song writing and Syd's, *Comfortably Numb: The Inside Story of Pink Floyd*, Mark Blake, 2008.

66

The Beatles loved the Floyd. We taught them everything they knew.

99

Nick Mason, on the Beatles, with a possible hint of sarcasm, *MOJO*, July 1995

QUADRAPHONIC PSYCHADELICS

Replacing Syd as leader of The Pink Floyd was OK. But Syd as a writer was a one-off. I could never aspire to his crazed insights and perceptions. In fact, for a long time I wouldn't have dreamt of claiming any insights whatsoever. But I'd always credit Syd with the connection he made to his personal unconscious and to the collective, group conscious.

Roger Waters, on replacing Syd as the de facto leader of the group in 1968, Q magazine, June 1987

When Syd flipped I had this theory that we could go on with Syd still being a member of the group if he could become Brian Wilson and simply be a backroom boy. But Syd had other ideas: he wanted to get in two sax-players and a girl singer. To which we resolutely said no!

Roger Waters, on his hopes of Syd remaining part of the band but assuming the sole role of songwriter, *Melody Maker*, 15 June 1987

QUADRAPHONIC PSYCHADELICS

The first plan was that I would join and make it a five piece so it would make it easier so that Syd could still be strange but the band would still function. And then the next idea was that Syd would stay home and do writing and be the Brian Wilson elusive character that didn't actually perform with us.

And the third plan was that he wouldn't do anything at all… it was obviously impossible to carry on working that way so we basically ditched Syd, [and] stopped picking him up for gigs.

David Gilmour, on leaving Syd out of the band, *The Source*, 1984

QUADRAPHONIC PSYCHADELICS

31 Tottenham Court Road, London

The original location of the UFO Club, the gig venue of which Pink Floyd were the resident house band from December 1966 to August 1967, where they played approximately 10 shows.

It was here that the Floyd established their earliest sound and stage show, for a counter-cultural crowd of avant-garde enthusiasts.

> We weren't loyal supporters of the underground… Yes, there was UFO, but for every UFO there were 20 gigs up the motorway at the Top Rank Ballroom, Dunstable, or whatever. The underground was a London event. By the time it moved out to the provinces it was much more a commercial enterprise, much more to do with the music than, perhaps, the intellectual aspirations. But for us, the buzz of being involved in the underground was enormously helpful.

Nick Mason, on Pink Floyd's involvement with the underground and psychedelic scene in London in the late 1960s, *MOJO*, July 1995

QUADRAPHONIC PSYCHADELICS

We could only play in London, because there the audience was more tolerant and was willing to withstand ten minutes of shit to discover five minutes of good music. We were at an experimental stage. We set out for unbelievable solos where no one would dare. The country audience wouldn't go through that.

Nick Mason, on London audiences compared to more regional audiences, March 1973

After Syd, Dave was the difference between light and dark. He was absolutely into form and shape and he introduced that into the wilder numbers we'd created. We became far less difficult to enjoy. And that made it more fun to play because you want to entertain, get some rapport going rather than antagonize. To annoy the audience beyond all reason is not my idea of a good night out.

Nick Mason, on the structure Dave bought to the group when he joined in 1968, *MOJO*, July 1995

QUADRAPHONIC PSYCHADELICS

I produced Syd's solo albums because I liked the songs, not, as I suppose some might think, because I felt guilty taking his place in the Floyd.

David Gilmour, on producing Syd's two solo albums *Barrett* and *The Madcap Laughs*, *NME*, 13 April 1974

I'm not thinking about the audience at all when I'm singing. I'm doing it entirely in my own head. Most of the time I shut my eyes and concentrate on speaking the words so that they mean what they're supposed to… It's vitally important that I do sing every syllable with meaning. You've got to believe it.

David Gilmour, on singing Roger's lyrics, as the group's lead singer, *MOJO*, July 1995

QUADRAPHONIC PSYCHADELICS

> **"**
> It was fairly obvious that I was brought in to take over from Syd. However, it was impossible to gauge his feelings about it. Syd functions on a totally different plane of logic, and some people will claim, 'Well, yeah man, he's on a higher cosmic level' – but basically there's something drastically wrong.
> **"**

David Gilmour, on assuming Syd's role in the group, and Syd's mental health decline, *NME*, 13 April 1974

> **"** I only know the thing of playing, of being a musician, was very exciting… One's position as a member of London's young people's underground wasn't necessarily realized especially from the point of view of groups. **"**

Syd Barrett, on the group's position as the pioneers of the London underground scene, *Melody Maker*, 27 March 1971

QUADRAPHONIC PSYCHADELICS

Syd was a casualty of the so-called Psychedelic Period that we were meant to represent. Everybody believed that we were taking acid before we went on stage and all that stuff. Unfortunately, one of us was, and that was Syd.

Roger Waters, on Syd's LSD use and decline as a live performer, *The Source*, 1984

PINK FLOYD

My initial ambition was just to get the band into some sort of shape. It seems ridiculous now, but I thought the band was awfully bad at the time when I joined. The gigs I'd seen with Syd were incredibly undisciplined. The leader figure was falling apart, and so was the band.

David Gilmour, on the state of Pink Floyd when David joined the group, *Rolling Stone*, 19 November 1987

QUADRAPHONIC PSYCHADELICS

❝

We were taken in to meet them once, while they were recording 'Lovely Rita'. It was a bit like meeting the Royal family.

❞

Nick Mason, on meeting the Beatles, who were recording at Abbey Road at the same time, *MOJO*, May 1994

PINK FLOYD

12 January 1968

The date David Gilmour made his debut as a member of Pink Floyd, at Aston University, Birmingham.

The band played five tracks:

"Set the Controls for the Heart of the Sun"

"Interstellar Overdrive"

"Flaming"

"Astronomy Domine"

"Pow R. Toc H."

QUADRAPHONIC PSYCHADELICS

I remember Nick and Roger drawing out *A Saucerful of Secrets* as an architectural diagram, in dynamic forms rather than in any sort of musical form, with peaks and troughs. That's what is was about. It wasn't music for beauty's sake, or for emotion's sake. It never had a storyline. Though for years afterwards we used to get letters from people saying what they thought it meant.

David Gilmour, on the creation of *A Saucerful of Secrets*, *MOJO*, May 1994

PINK FLOYD

Syd had been my friend at Cambridge Tech, where we'd swap guitar tips… We'd also spent one summer busking around France together. Obviously, I felt both shy and nervous about replacing him. Apparently, I spent a lot of 1968 with my back to the audience.

David Gilmour, on replacing Syd, *MOJO*, October 2007

QUADRAPHONIC PSYCHADELICS

The body of work that the four of us produced together post-Syd has some of that connection to the same things that the Beatles' work has a connection to, and that for me makes Pink Floyd important. And to continue with Gilmour and Mason, getting in a whole bunch of other people to write the material, seems to me an insult to the work that came before. And that's why I wanted the name to retire.

Roger Waters, on wanting Pink Floyd to cease altogether after he and his creative leadership left the band, *MOJO*, December 1999

PINK FLOYD

There were fights, but we did have really good times. We were unsuccessful at putting humour across. We put some great jokes in things, little backwards messages to pander to these anoraks who hunt for things and claim malign influences. We had vast amounts of fun doing that. But no one seemed to spot it.

David Gilmour, on inserting jokes and humour into their songs for fans to pick up on, *The Guardian*, 25 October 2002

QUADRAPHONIC PSYCHADELICS

> "[Peter Jenner and Andrew King – Floyd's managers] thought Syd and I were the musical brains of the group, and that we should form a break-away band, to try to hold Syd together. He and I were living together in a flat in Richmond at the time. And believe me, I would have left with him like a shot if I thought Syd could do it."

David Gilmour, on forming a new group with Syd, *MOJO*, May 1994

It wasn't really a war. I suppose it was really just a matter of being a little offhand about things… I don't think The Pink Floyd had any trouble, but I had an awful scene, probably self-inflicted.

Syd Barrett, when asked "Why did you leave the group?", *Melody Maker*, 27 March 1971

QUADRAPHONIC PSYCHADELICS

Yes, hippies used to be a large part of our audience, but I don't think even Syd or I were hippies. In fact, none of us believed in the hippy philosophy. We were part of a wider movement that was all about freedom. And freedom for me meant we can actually go on stage and make these weird sounds, and people are gonna listen and pay you for it!

Rick Wright, on the hippy era of the late 1960s, *MOJO*, October 2007

> We were so blinkered. I maintain that we looked after Syd very badly – but we didn't know any better. There's still the belief that it was LSD damage, but it could have been perfectly straightforward, that he wanted to be an artist and not a pop star. And actually, that could break you, and certainly not do you any good at all to be forced down a road you didn't want to go.

Nick Mason, on the group's treatment of Syd as his mental health declined, *Uncut*, 14 March 2017

QUADRAPHONIC PSYCHADELICS

> I'm disappearing. I'm treading the backward path. Mostly, I just waste my time. I'm sorry I can't speak very coherently. It's rather difficult to think of anybody being really interested in me. But you know, man, I am totally together. I don't think I'm easy to talk about. I've got a very irregular head. And I'm not anything that you think I am anyway.

Syd Barrett, on his state of mental decline, *Rolling Stone*, December 1971

You must never underestimate how unpopular we were around the rest of England. They hated it. They would throw things, pour beer over us. And we were terrible, though we didn't quite know it. Promoters were always coming up to us and saying, 'I don't know why you boys won't do proper songs.' Looking back on it, I can't think why we persevered.

Nick Mason, on touring London in the late 1960s, and how disinterested the rest of England were in underground psychedelia, *MOJO*, May 1994

QUADRAPHONIC PSYCHADELICS

Dave Gilmour was brought in because we knew he could sing and we knew he could play the guitar, which was what we badly needed. We also thought he was someone we could get on with. It's probably more important to get people you can get on with than it is to get good musicians. That's certainly true of us. I think the reason we're still running is because, after a fashion, we can all live together.

Nick Mason, on David Gilmour as Syd's replacement, *NME*, 19 February 1972

In all honesty, psychedelia had been a bloody good launch pad, but it was not something we felt comfortable with. It was tied in with all these hippy concepts – love, crystals and all the rest of it. Whereas we were heading down this darker road, towards *Dark Side…* which is a very technical piece about much more introverted ideas. It soon seemed quite important that we lose the tripping-on-acid image.

Nick Mason, on the "psychedelic" tag that hounded the band in their earlier days, *MOJO*, October 2007

CHAPTER
THREE

HIGH HOPES

From 1969 to 1973, Pink Floyd released a series of highly respected records – *More*, *Ummagumma*, *Atom Heart Mother*, *Meddle* and *Obscured By Clouds* – which increased their British and European fanbase away from the confines of the UK capital city.

Pink Floyd, beloved by the Beatles and their peers, had left Earth's orbit and were on the lookout for their next destination…

HIGH HOPES

"
We all like our music. That's the only driving force behind us. All the trappings of becoming vaguely successful like being able to buy bigger amplifiers – none of that stuff is really important.
"

Roger Waters, on playing in unsuitable venus, *Melody Maker*, 5 August 1967

> I'd say the transition between *Ummagumma* and *Atom Heart Mother* was the most important… At the time I thought we were making the most incredible music in the world, but looking back it wasn't so good.

Rick Wright, on the band's evolution of sound and technique during their earlier albums, *MOJO*, July 1995

HIGH HOPES

I had no idea that I would ever write anything when I bought my first guitar at age 15 and decided that I was going to be a rock star along with umpteen million other kids. I had no idea that I would ever really write songs, and in the early years, I didn't have to because Syd was writing all the material. It was only after he stopped writing that the rest of us had to start trying to do it.

Roger Waters, on his earliest song writing efforts for the group, *The Source*, 1984

PINK FLOYD

Pink Floyd is bigger than the three of us and it was bigger than the four of us. Back in the 70s people came to hear the music and see the show, not to see [us] as personalities jumping around onstage. Even in UFO days people came for the experience – the lights plus the music. We were happy not to be in the limelight.

Rick Wright, on the faceless anonymity of the members of Pink Floyd in relation to their importance to the band as a whole, *MOJO*, July 1995

HIGH HOPES

The day we were trying to think of the album title, we had a newspaper, sitting outside a pub in London, in our break in recording, 7 o'clock on a sunny evening in London, and there was a woman who had had heart surgery, and had an atomic heart pacemaker fitted on her heart, and she was a mother. It said 'Atom Heart Mother blah blah blah...' We thought 'Atom Heart Mother... title!' Simple as that.

David Gilmour, on the naming of the album *Atom Heart Mother*, *The Source*, 1984

> All I've ever tried to do is play music that I like listening to. Some of it now, like *Atom Heart Mother*, strikes me as absolute crap.

David Gilmour, talking about *Atom Heart Mother*, Q magazine, November 1994

HIGH HOPES

Artists simply do feel and see things in a different way to other people. In a way it's a blessing, but it can also be a terrible curse.

Roger Waters, on the burdens of being a creative artist, *Melody Maker*, 15 June 1987

Albums

1. *The Piper at the Gates of Dawn* — 1967
2. *A Saucerful of Secrets* — 1968
3. *More* — 1969
4. *Ummagumma* — 1969
5. *Atom Heart Mother* — 1970
6. *Meddle* — 1971
7. *Obscured By Clouds* — 1972
8. *The Dark Side of the Moon* — 1973
9. *Wish You Were Here* — 1975
10. *Animals* — 1977
11. *The Wall* — 1979
12. *The Final Cut* — 1983
13. *A Momentary Lapse of Reason* — 1987
14. *The Division Bell* — 1994
15. *The Endless River* — 2014

HIGH HOPES

I saw this huge… bald, fat guy, I thought, 'He looks a bit… strange.' I sat down with Roger at the desk and this guy kept on getting up and brushing his teeth and then sitting – doing really weird things. . . suddenly I realized it was Syd, after maybe 45 minutes. He came in as we were doing the vocals for 'Shine On You Crazy Diamond', which was basically about Syd.

He just for some incredible reason picked the very day that we were doing a song about him. And we hadn't seen him… for two years before.

❞

Rick Wright, on Syd's surprise appearance in the studio during the recording of "Shine On You Crazy Diamond", a song about Syd, *The Source*, 1984

HIGH HOPES

The most Floydian material we ever did, like 'Echoes', came about that way would be all of us in a rehearsal room, just sitting there thinking, playing, working out ideas to see if they went anywhere. It's a nice way to work.

Rick Wright, on his preference to songwriting collaboration, *Rolling Stone*, November 19, 1987

PINK FLOYD

"
There was no point in Gilmour, Mason or Wright trying to write lyrics. Because they'll never be as good as mine. Gilmour's lyrics are very third-rate. And in comparison with what I do, I'm sure he'd agree. He's just not as good. I didn't play the guitar solos; he didn't write any lyrics.
"

Roger Waters, on the group's lyric writing, *Rolling Stone*, November 19, 1987

HIGH HOPES

I've got to recognize the really weird fans, who get there at six o'clock, grab their place at the front, take all the drugs and then, just as we start playing, they keel over.

Nick Mason, on the group's superfans, Q magazine, November 1994

Horseplay? [There were] thousands of incidents. I remember the time Dave drove a motorbike into a restaurant and out again – in a very straight bit of America – and most of the diners pretended it wasn't happening.

Rick Wright, on the band's off-duty behaviour when touring, Q magazine, November 1994

Lulubelle III

The name of the now-iconic cow on the band's 1970 album, *Atom Heart Mother*.

The cover was created by genius-level Hipgnosis designers, and friends of the band, Storm Thorgerson and Aubrey Powell.

PINK FLOYD

They attach far too much importance to us. Some obsessives think we're in control of something they don't understand or we have some telephone line to the powers that be. We make music to stimulate and entertain. We make it as deep and meaningful as we can, but it's only pop music.

David Gilmour, on Pink Floyd's fans and their hero worship of the band, *USA Today*, 1994

HIGH HOPES

At Abbey Road, there were three sessions a day: nine to twelve, two 'til five and then seven 'til ten. The Beatles had special dispensation to go beyond those times, though. When we made *Piper*, we renegotiated our contract so that we took a smaller percentage but had unlimited studio time, which probably was silly. There's nothing like knowing you've got unlimited studio time to go, 'Oh, let's sit around playing cards.'

Nick Mason, on recording their debut album at Abbey Road, *Uncut*, 14 March 2017

Ummagumma was absolutely not a band album. We were looking for new ways of constructing an album, although I think what this demonstrates is that our sum is always better than the parts.

Nick Mason, on the recording of *Ummagumma*, *MOJO*, May 1994

HIGH HOPES

> **"**
> Sometimes during the day I'll get this very blank feeling – not an empty feeling, it's very full – and I'll realize suddenly that I'm really long-sighted, everything becomes very out-of-focus, and I think, 'Oh, I'm going to write a song.'
> **"**

Roger Waters, on his song writing process, *MOJO*, December 1999

We're not well-known for our duck-walking and gyrating about onstage.

Nick Mason, on the band's need for a huge stage show to balance out the band's lack of onstage movement and interaction, *MOJO*, December 1999

HIGH HOPES

None of us recognized him. He'd put on about four stone, shaved off all his body hair, and he was eating a big bag of sweets.

Roger Waters, about Syd's drastic change in appearance since he was last seen by anyone, *The Guardian*, 23 April 2001

PINK FLOYD

> **"**
> At the time, people were always looking for messages in our albums. So we thought: 'Oh, well. We better do one.' It's complete nonsense.
> **"**

Nick Mason, about the backward messages* the band created on songs to confuse and excite fans, *Sonic Reality*, 6 March 2014

* Roger Waters can be heard speaking when "Empty Spaces" is played backwards: "Congratulations. You've just discovered the secret message. Please send your answer to Old Pink, care of the funny farm, Chalfont."

HIGH HOPES

We were never a band of brothers, I don't think, more a band of seekers. We were people dedicated to hunting down and playing something with meaning and soul.

David Gilmour, *Classic Rock* magazine, 4 December 2002

I think Roger's lyrics are extraordinary, because I think they are as relevant, if not more relevant, to a 50- or 60-year-old, than to a 20-something year old.

Nick Mason, on the quality of Roger's lyric writing, *Planet Rock Radio*, 22 March 2013

HIGH HOPES

If you make a mistake, always glare at the bass player.

Nick Mason, when asked "What's the best advice you've ever received?", Q magazine, August 1995

We don't see Syd, because apparently if he's ever reminded of Pink Floyd and when he was in it, he goes into a depression for weeks on end. His mother asked us to stay away a few years ago. Apparently, most of the time he's quite happy – or was – but our faces can trigger off a lapse.

Rick Wright, on Syd, and his inability to discuss Pink Floyd, *Observer*, 22 April 2001

CHAPTER FOUR

LUNAR LUNACY

With 1973's *The Dark Side of the Moon*, Pink Floyd became the biggest-selling band of the decade.

Perhaps the first-ever fully realized concept album, *Dark Side* explored lyrical themes that resonated with listeners all over world, soundtracked by some of the most innovative pieces of music ever committed to vinyl.

The album was the sound of the future, and is revealed in all its glory here…

LUNAR LUNACY

Dark Side of the Moon finished the Pink Floyd off once and for all. To be that successful is the aim of every group. And once you've cracked it, it's all over.

Roger Waters, on the curse of *The Dark Side of the Moon*'s success, *Melody Maker*, 15 June 1987

> The concept grew out of group discussions about the pressures of real life, like travel or money, but then Roger broadened it into a meditation on the causes of insanity.

Nick Mason, on the concept behind *The Dark Side of the Moon*, *MOJO*, May 1994

LUNAR LUNACY

> Yes, it is nice isn't it? We've never really been above fortieth position before.

David Gilmour, on the staggering success of *The Dark Side of the Moon*, NME, 19 May 1973

PINK FLOYD

We thought we could do a whole thing about the pressures we personally feel that drive one over the top… the pressure of earning a lot of money; time flying by very fast; organized power structures like the church or politics; violence; aggression. The whole album is about the way modern life leads to madness.

Roger Waters, on the themes of *The Dark Side of the Moon*, *Saucerful of Secrets: The Pink Floyd Odyssey* by Nicholas Schaffner, 1991

LUNAR LUNACY

In 1972, British heavy blues rockers Medicine Head released an album called *Dark Side of the Moon*. This prompted Pink Floyd to change the name of their forthcoming new album to *Eclipse*.

However, when Medicine Head's album slipped into obscurity, Floyd reinstated *The Dark Side of the Moon** as the album's title, and the rest is history.

* The album's title is a reference to lunacy, not space.

It's difficult to plunge yourself back into parallel lifetimes of a long time ago, parts of which you don't feel comfortable remembering.

David Gilmour, on looking back at the creation of *The Dark Side of the Moon* on its 40th anniversary, *Rolling Stone*, 27 June 2016

LUNAR LUNACY

Storm and Po's [from Hipgnosis] record sleeve was absolutely right. People sometimes ask about that – they came into the studio to show us their ideas. We saw the prism and said, 'We like that.' They said 'No, no, we've got others,' but we said, 'No, no, we don't want to see others, we like that!'

Nick Mason, on Hipgnosis's prism design for the cover of *The Dark Side of the Moon* being immediately beloved by the band, *Planet Rock Radio*, 22 March 2013

It's very well balanced and well constructed, dynamically and musically, and I think the humanity of its approach is appealing. I think also that it was the first album of that kind, the first completely cohesive concept album that was made.

Roger Waters, on why *The Dark Side of the Moon* was such a colossally successful record, *Melody Maker*, 15 June 1987

> *Dark Side* comes higher in my estimation, partly because it was more pleasurable – we were all interacting; a true collaborative effort. But *The Wall* is an extraordinary piece of work. Some things I don't like, like Roger moaning about his wife. But I think it still stands up today.

Nick Mason, on his complaints about *The Wall*, *Record Collector*, March 2000

The big difference for me with *Dark Side* was the fact that we'd played it live before we recorded it. You couldn't do that now of course, you'd be bootlegged out of existence. But when we went into the studio we all knew the material. The playing was very good. It had a natural feel. And it was a bloody good package. The music, the concept, the cover, all came together.

David Gilmour, on the concept and creation of *The Dark Side of the Moon*, *MOJO*, May 1994

LUNAR LUNACY

We'd cracked it. We'd won the pools. What are you supposed to do after that? *Dark Side of the Moon* was the last willing collaboration: after that, everything with the band was like drawing a teeth; 10 years of hanging on to the married name and not having the courage to get divorced, to let go; 10 years of bloody hell. It was all just terrible. Awful. Terrible.

Roger Waters, on his divorce from Pink Floyd, Q magazine, November 1992

> When it was finished, I took the tape home and played it to my first wife, and I remember her bursting into tears when she'd finished listening to it. And I thought, yeah, that's kind of what I expected, because I think it's very moving emotionally and musically. Maybe its humanity has caused *Dark Side* to last as long as it has.

Roger Waters, on *The Dark Side of the Moon*'s enduring legacy, *Washington Post*, 28 April 1992

LUNAR LUNACY

Looking at it now, there are two particular reasons for its success. First of all the album went out at a particularly right moment. The second reason for the success of the album is that when it became such a success, people bought it because of that.

Nick Mason, on why *The Dark Side of the Moon* was so successful, *Ciao 2001* magazine, 25 May 1975

Dark Side was actually an enormously undruggy affair but abstract enough for people to read all sorts of things into it. So it gave us a flavour of being this freaky band, and it just stuck around. With that album, everybody fell into their roles and knew what to do. You can't get on that badly when you're sharing rooms and driving in one car. It's different when you can afford four limos and charter jets. Bands inevitably work together well until they achieve something, which is the catalyst for the big explosion.

Nick Mason, on the recording and success of *The Dark Side of the Moon*, *Maxim* magazine, January 2002

LUNAR LUNACY

After *Dark Side of the Moon* we had a bit of money and I bought a house in the country – I had two young children. Roger sat down and said to me, 'I can't believe you've done this, you've sold out, I think it's disgusting.' Six months later he went and bought a much bigger house in the country. I said, 'Remember what you said?' He said, 'Ah yes, but that's because my wife wanted it, not me.' Absolute bullshit. I found him rather hypocritical. That's what angered me about him.

Rick Wright, on Roger being a hypocrite when concerning matters of the material world, *MOJO*, July 1995.

250 Million

The combined total album sales of Pink Floyd's 15 studio albums.

The Dark Side of the Moon has sold more than 45 million copies, the fourth biggest-selling album of all time.

LUNAR LUNACY

> I'm putting my life's blood into it. But Pink Floyd is not only me. I am bound by other people's desires and choices and politics and needs. The whole thing is a constant compromise of ideals and art all the way through.

David Gilmour, on the complex power dynamics at the heart of operating Pink Floyd, *MOJO*, July 1995

PINK FLOYD

Your writing comes out largely from a personality that develops when you're a child. And that how successful you may become, you don't change inside. You may become crushed by the weight of your success, and that weight may prevent you from expressing the feelings that you will always have inside, but I don't think that the way a person feels ever really changes through their life. Do you?

Roger Waters, on songwriting and success, *The Source*, 1984

LUNAR LUNACY

Our music has depth, and attempts philosophical thought and meaning with discussions of infinity, eternity and mortality. There is a line which people cross that turns it into some magical, mystical realm, for which I don't claim responsibility and don't hold any great truck with.

David Gilmour, on the perceived mystical qualities of the group's timeless music, *Record Collector*, May 2003

It's a lovely thing to see a new generation in our audience, the kids of people who used to see us. There are people who say we should make room for younger bands. That's not the way it works. They can make their own room.

David Gilmour, on being a band with pan-generational appeal and on young bands coming up, *USA Today*, 1994

LUNAR LUNACY

I'm amazed that people who weren't born when we started making records know all our old records.

Rick Wright, on remaining a band with pan-generational appeal, *USA Today*, 1994

PINK FLOYD

> Who? Never heard of him. Is he one of them rappers? Leave me alone. I've got to get some coleslaw.

Syd Barrett, his last words on record, when asked "Are you Syd Barrett?", 23 April 2001

LUNAR LUNACY

I'm obsessed with truth and how the futile scramble for material things obscures our possible path to understanding ourselves, each other and the universe in ways that will make human life more fulfilling for all human beings. That's what *Dark Side of the Moon* is about, and what most of my records have been about.

Roger Waters, on the themes of his songwriting, *Washington Post*, 28 April 1992

I'm not famous; I'm a part of a famous enterprise, which is rather different. Most genuinely famous people seem to be driven by the notion that fame will make them feel better, and when it doesn't they try and plug that gap with more fame. So yes, Pink Floyd are desperately damaged individuals and we're just not famous enough yet!

Nick Mason, on fame, Q magazine, August 1995

LUNAR LUNACY

Quality. Universal themes. I can understand it. It's good stuff. People listen to Neil Young and Joni Mitchell the same way. We're in a fine, select group it's great for every new generation to investigate. I'm happy to be considered part of it.

David Gilmour, on the secret behind Pink Floyd's pan-generational appeal, *Record Collector*, May 2003

> That's one of the most ludicrous things, and it just runs and runs and runs. I mean, we're obviously to blame for some of these stupid things ourselves, but God knows where that one came from… I did try it once, actually. It didn't seem to make any sense whatsoever. I wouldn't bother. It's better to listen to the words rather than to find out about little Dorothy and her red shoes!

David Gilmour, on the myth that *The Dark Side of the Moon* syncs up perfectly with *The Wizard Of Oz*, *Record Collector*, May 2003

LUNAR LUNACY

> Herbie Hancock did one of our songs, Eric Prydz did too, I like it when people reinterpret something. That's great. What bothers me are tribute bands who practise every stick I've ever dropped.

Nick Mason, on the wide-ranging quality of Pink Floyd tribute bands*, interview with Mark Jeeves, Planet Rock Radio, 22 March 2013

* "One thing I really like about the best-known tribute band, the Australian Pink Floyd, is that they eventually split due to musical differences – you'd have thought that they'd have seen that coming!" said Nick Mason, about Pink Floyd's most famous tribute band.

You'll never get me to take this stuff seriously. However hard you try, it's not gonna happen, OK? I refuse to take any of it seriously. We were just young guys getting together, wanting to be rich and get laid.

Roger Waters, on the hero worship the band receives from its legion of loyal fans as a result of *Dark Side*'s success, *MOJO*, October 2007

LUNAR LUNACY

> My doctor said never play above your pulse rate.

Nick Mason, on his drumming style and technique, *Rolling Stone*, 13 October 2011

❝

We lost a couple of million quid – everything we'd made from *Dark Side of the Moon*. Then we discovered the Inland Revenue might come and ask us for 83 per cent of the money we had lost. Which we didn't have. We had gone from fourteen-years-olds with ten quid guitars and fantasies of being rich and famous, and made the dream come true with *Dark Side of the Moon*, and then, being greedy and trying to protect it, we'd lost it all.

❞

Roger Waters, on the band's infamous tax problems, and exile, after *The Dark Side of the Moon*'s success, *Melody Maker*, 15 June 1987

CHAPTER FIVE

MIND CONTROL

What goes up, must come down. After the unparalleled global praise of *The Dark Side of the Moon*, Pink Floyd had become too big to control.

With *Wish You Were Here*, *Animals*, *The Wall* and *The Final Cut*, the scars of Pink Floyd's success were all too visible to see.

The once luminous group began to splinter and an increasing sense of implosion occurred with each new album until it all became too much… and Pink Floyd went supernova.

MIND CONTROL

In stadiums, the more the merrier, the sound surrounding you, fireworks, anything that stops them playing frisbee at the back is a good thing.

Nick Mason, on the band's iconic use of stage props and pyrotechnics during stadium gigs, *MOJO*, July 1995

> During *Animals* was when it started to come to a head for me. Roger was changing, he really did believe that he was the leader of the band, he really did believe that it was only because of him that the band was still going. And, obviously, when he started developing his ego trips, the person he would have his conflicts with would be me.

Rick Wright, on his now-legendary fall out with Roger that led to Rick being "fired" from the group, *MOJO*, July 1995

MIND CONTROL

> The idea for *The Wall* came from 10 years of touring and rock shows… particularly the last few years in '75 and in '77 we were playing to very large audiences some of whom were our old audience who'd come to see us play, but most of whom were only there for the beer, in big stadiums, and consequently it became rather an alienating experience… I became very conscious of a wall between us and our audience and so this record started out as being an expression of those feelings.

Roger Waters, on the lyrical themes in *The Wall*, speaking to Tommy Vance on *Radio 1*, 1979

PINK FLOYD

> My therapist is convinced I'm still extremely angry about the whole thing and in a sense I am. I think it was nasty. This is my band as much as it's his… Hopefully one day I'll sit down with Roger and he might then say, 'Yes, it was unfair.'

Rick Wright, on being asked to leave Pink Floyd (at Roger's insistence), *MOJO*, December 1999

MIND CONTROL

I don't share Roger's sense of angst about music and the world. If I did, maybe we would have come to an agreement on our dispute.

David Gilmour, on Roger and his difference of opinion that led to their legal issues about Pink Floyd ownership, *Penthouse* magazine, September 1988

PINK FLOYD

I thought the Sex Pistols were rather good. I've been on a show with Johnny Rotten… and he said he never really hated Pink Floyd and actually he was a bit of a fan. I confess to not having entirely believed it in the first place. I mean, who could hate us?

David Gilmour, on the Sex Pistols [who famously wore "I Hate Pink Floyd" T-shirts], *Q* magazine, June 1999

MIND CONTROL

As I saw it, Roger's original concept for the show was literally to build a wall, go home and leave the audience pissed off.

Rick Wright, on Roger's vision for the original *The Wall* stadium tour of 1980-81, *MOJO*, December 1999

Following Roger's Toronto incident [a fan in the front row kept screaming; it drove Roger crazy enough to spit at him]… [Roger] came to us afterwards and said he wanted to start the set with us playing as normal, then build a wall across in front of us. I completely disagreed. I said… people would hate it. Which I think was part of the idea, he wanted people to hate it.

Rick Wright, on the origin of *The Wall* concept, *MOJO*, July 1995

MIND CONTROL

There was no studio interference because there was no studio; none of them would give us any money. We turned to rock stars for finance. Elton John, Pink Floyd, Led Zeppelin, they all had money, they knew our work and we seemed a good tax write-off. Except, of course, we weren't.

Terry Gilliam, director of *Monty Python and the Holy Grail**, *The Guardian*, 2002

* Pink Floyd were huge fans of Monty Python. So much so, the group funded the troupe's first feature film, the brilliantly absurd 1975 quest, *Monty Python and the Holy Grail*, with more than £21,000 pounds, one-tenth of the entire film's budget

---

The meaning of it was Roger's story. He was the one who strongly felt that wall between himself and our audience.
I have never entirely gone along with that… I think I relate to the audience a lot more than Roger thinks he does. That's the accurate way to put it.

David Gilmour, on the symbolism of *The Wall* and Pink Floyd's relationship with their fans, *MOJO*, July 1995

MIND CONTROL

> Someone did suggest that if we altered the design of the pig then Roger couldn't claim it. A pig's a pig, for Christ's sake. How do you alter its design? You add testicles. Well, it was amusing for us.

David Gilmour, on adding testicles to the large inflatable stage prop pig to ensure they could use it live without infringing intellectual property rights, *MOJO*, July 1995

My one pathetic victory was that they had to put testicles on the pig. If the pig had been exactly the same as the pig that I designed, I could have stopped them using it in their shows. So they put balls on my pig. Fuck them.

Roger Waters, on his bitter dispute over the name Pink Floyd with David and Nick, *Q magazine*, November 1992

MIND CONTROL

The concept (of *The Wall*'s theme influencing its author's behaviour) is a convenient view for people. It's a short step from leader to dictator. We're all volunteers. Nobody had to stay… We'd been arguing since 1974, for God's sake. Too long. At a certain point you have to say, this is not working, the point has come to break up.

Roger Waters, on the break down of band relationships during *The Wall* and *The Final Cut* and his decision to exit the group, *MOJO*, December 1999

PINK FLOYD

We were touring *Wish You Were Here* in Pennsylvania and were playing under this inflatable pyramid… Sure enough, it was raining with winds of 28 mph, and it took off, then inverted above the stadium. A helium pod fell out, and someone yelled, 'My God, it's giving birth!' It then fell back to earth, fortunately not killing anyone underneath.

Nick Mason, on the stage construction and props for the US tour of *Wish You Were Here*, *Maxim* magazine, January 2002

MIND CONTROL

> **"**
> I just went out into the studio and banged out five or six solos.
> **"**

David Gilmour, on the creation of the iconic "Comfortably Numb" guitar solo, *Guitar World*, February 1993

I would be distressed if Paul McCartney and Ringo Starr made records and went on the road calling themselves the Beatles. If John Lennon's not in it, it's sacrilegious.

Roger Waters, on Pink Floyd remaining a group without him as a member, *MOJO*, December 1999

MIND CONTROL

> **"**
> I said to Roger, 'If these songs weren't good enough for *The Wall*, why are they good enough for now?' We had the most awful time of my life. Roger had got Rick out, Nick wasn't around much and now he was starting on me. A most unpleasant and humiliating experience.
> **"**

David Gilmour, on the recording struggles with Roger for *The Final Cut*, *MOJO*, May 1994

If Roger could've done it all by himself he would have. He may have thought he could take the bat and ball away, but his leaving revitalized us. Going back on tour without knowing whether the public would still accept us was exciting. It was like being in a band again.

Nick Mason, on recording *The Final Cut*, *Maxim* magazine, January 2002

MIND CONTROL

I don't analyze too much who was the heart, who was the brains, who was the soul. All I can say is it was a pop group and it had a sound, and the bass player doesn't usually create the whole sound, does he? One could say, if it was all Roger, why hasn't he done better since? But I wouldn't say that. I will not allow myself to get drawn in.

David Gilmour, on not being drawn into who did what in Pink Floyd, *The Guardian*, 25 October 2002

PINK FLOYD

> I wrote *The Wall* as an attack on stadium rock – and there's 'Pink Floyd' making money out of it by playing it in stadiums! They have to bear the cross of that betrayal. They have to live with the denial of what the work was about. But when all that nonsense started, it made me fucking gloomy. I stood by a river and stared at myself in the water. Pathetic, I said. They despoiled my creations and there was nothing I could do about it.

Roger Waters, on the irony of David, Rick and Nick performing *The Wall* songs live at stadiums after Roger had left the band, *Q* magazine, November 1992

MIND CONTROL

There was this band meeting in which Roger told me he wanted me to leave the band. At first I refused. So Roger stood up and said that if I didn't agree to leave after the album was finished, he would walk out then and there and take the tapes with him. There would be no album, and no money to pay off our huge debts. So I agreed to go. I had two young kids to support. I was terrified.

Rick Wright, on leaving the band at Roger's insistence, *MOJO*, May 1994

I went out to dinner with Rick after Roger had [asked him to leave] and said if he wanted to stay in the band I would support him in that. I did point out to Rick that he hadn't contributed anything of any value whatsoever to the album and that I was not over-happy with him myself… but his position in the band to me was sacrosanct.

David Gilmour, on Roger's decision to fire Rick from the band, *MOJO*, December 1999

MIND CONTROL

I would never have imagined that we could have carried on without Roger until Dave said, 'We can. Let's have a go.' The feeling was, it's not your band to kill.

Nick Mason, on continuing onwards with Pink Floyd without Roger at the helm, *MOJO*, December 1999

> [Stadium gigs] just became more and more oppressive. Those places weren't built for music, they were built for sporting events, and it's not unnatural to experience a ritualization of war, because that's all sport is. What was going through my mind – my whole body – was an enormous sense of frustration, a feeling of what are we all doing here, what's the point? And the answer that kept clanging back monotonously was: cash and ego. That's all it's about.

Roger Waters, on touring stadium gigs, *The Wall* and his motivations to leave the group, *MOJO*, December 1999

MIND CONTROL

I came to see it as one of the luckiest people in the world issuing a catalogue of abuse and bile against people who'd never done anything to him.

David Gilmour, on Roger and the meaning behind *The Wall*, *The Times*, 30 June 2006

> Roger wanted to do all the writing, he wanted to take over the whole thing. He would engineer moments to try and ensure that no one else got any writing. Certainly on *The Final Cut*, he engineered a situation where no one else could do any writing.

David Gilmour, on Roger's dictatorial style of leading the band in their last few years, *Creem*, February 1988

MIND CONTROL

There will always be people who feel that Pink Floyd finished when Roger left, just as there are people who feel Pink Floyd ended when Syd Barrett left. And you can't change that for them, as much as I would love to be able to, sort of, convince them otherwise.

Nick Mason, on fans' reactions to band members leaving the group, DJ Redbeard radio interview, 30 March 1994

The Wall album was not a Roger Waters solo album, no matter what anyone thinks. It was a year of very hard work by Roger and all of us, turning a good idea that can only be described as a pig's ear, into a silk purse.

David Gilmour, on *The Wall* being a group effort, *Creem*, February 1988

MIND CONTROL

We spent 18 years touring with people shouting, 'Where's Syd Barrett?' but so far we haven't had one person shout, 'Where's Roger?'

Nick Mason, on fan reactions to Roger's exiting of the group, *Creem*, February 1988

The general rule of thumb is that the reason why bands stay together is because the sum is greater than the parts... that as long as all the members of the band feel that... they can achieve more together than they can on their own, there is a purpose to the band remaining together. And the reason why people leave bands is because they no longer believe that to be the case.

Nick Mason, on the reason he believes Roger quit the group, DJ Redbeard radio interview, 30 March 1994

MIND CONTROL

What we have is a record contract that very specifically says that if one of us leaves, the deal is still with Pink Floyd… What happened was Roger wrote to the record company and said he's leaving. So Pink Floyd was still understood to be whoever remained… He invoked the leaving member clause: if he leaves the band, it gives him a solo record contract.

Nick Mason, on Roger leaving the group, *Creem*, February 1988

There is no doubt that we lost a major contributor, talent or whatever when Roger left, but what's been very interesting has been the way it's galvanized us to do things that we would never have done if Roger had stayed.

Nick Mason, on Roger leaving the group, *Creem*, February 1988

MIND CONTROL

I remember meetings in which Roger said, 'You'll never fucking do it.' That's precisely what was said. Exactly that term. Except slightly harder.

David Gilmour, on calling Roger's bluff that his exit would be the de facto end of the group, *Rolling Stone*, 19 November 1987

The story that gets out is that it was a personal whim of mine, which is absolute bollocks.

Roger Waters, on the motivations behind firing Rick from the group, *Rolling Stone*, 19 November 1987

MIND CONTROL

Well, you lost something and you gain something. Frankly, at this moment I think we gained more than we lost. Our memories of our time with Roger are sort of tempered by the last few years, and the last few years have… been torture. The thought of continuing with Roger in that frame of mind was far worse than the thought of him going.

David Gilmour, on Roger leaving the group, interview with *Creem*, February 1988

Making *The Final Cut* was the final straw. I was virtually the only one in the studio and the others just didn't seem to care… The name Pink Floyd should have died then.

Roger Waters, on the recording of *The Final Cut*, Roger's last album under the name Pink Floyd, *MOJO*, March 2003

CHAPTER SIX

COMFORTABLY FAMOUS

Among the bitterness of the group's fallout out with each other, Pink Floyd (without Roger) released two thrilling albums, *A Momentary Lapse of Reason* and *The Division Bell*, before Rick Wright's untimely death in 2008, just after the band reunited one final time for Live 8 in 2005. (*The Endless River* [2014], the band's last record, is a tribute to him.)

Let's take one last trip down *Arnold Layne* and remember the band as they deserve: as pioneers of a new frontier…

COMFORTABLY FAMOUS

Once you've had that guitar up so loud on the stage, where you can lean back and volume will stop you from falling backward, that's a hard drug to kick.

David Gilmour, on his love of performing live, *Rolling Stone*, 13 October 2011

PINK FLOYD

Roger left in 1985. I was in my late thirties and I'd joined Pink Floyd when I was 21. My entire adult life had been working on this artistic enterprise, this band, which was pretty much playing the sort of music that I loved. Why would I suddenly want to quit? I didn't want to quit. The fact is for me, we went on, we continued doing what we did, we were pretty damn successful at it, and had a fantastic great time.

David Gilmour, on carrying on with the band after Roger quit, *Rolling Stone*, 13 October 2011

At the rehearsal, things were very tense. Roger had written a set list of songs he wanted to do, which I found entirely inappropriate for a charity event. Singing 'We don't need no education' just didn't do it for me. We did have to gently remind Roger that he was guesting in our band.

David Gilmour, on the band's tense reunion for Live 8 in 2005, *Rolling Stone*, 13 October 2011

We never sat down at any point and said, 'It doesn't sound Floyd enough. Make this more Floyd.' We just worked on the songs until they sounded right. When they sounded great and right, that's when it became Pink Floyd.

David Gilmour, on the recording of *A Momentary Lapse of Reason*, *Penthouse* magazine, September 1988

> **I have nothing against Dave Gilmour furthering his own goals. It's just the idea of Dave's solo career masquerading as Pink Floyd that offends me!**

Roger Waters, on David's continuation of Pink Floyd after he quit, interview with *Penthouse* magazine, September 1988

[Are our album and stage props art or bollocks?] I do know that there is no way a big inflatable pig can be mentioned in the same breath as Van Gogh's yellow chair. I wish to make that quite clear.

Nick Mason, on the band's iconic album artwork and stage props, *MOJO*, July 1995

COMFORTABLY FAMOUS

> **If one of us was going to be called Pink Floyd, it's me.**

Roger Waters, on David securing the Pink Floyd name after Roger quit, *Rolling Stone*, 19 November 1987

He forced his way to become the central figure. We could have been making better records if Roger had been willing to back off a little, to be more open to other people's input.

David Gilmour, on Roger taking control of the band, *Rolling Stone*, 19 November 1987

COMFORTABLY FAMOUS

"
Even Roger says what a miserable period it was. And he was the one who entirely made it miserable, in my opinion.
"

David Gilmour, on the misery caused by Roger's leadership during *The Wall* and *The Final Cut*, *Rolling Stone*, 19 November 1987

It is frustrating to find out how many people don't know who I am or what I actually did in Pink Floyd. We get on a plane, and people ask what band we're in. I tell them I'm Roger Waters, and it doesn't mean a thing to them. Then I mention Pink Floyd, and they go, 'Yeah, "Money". I love *The Wall*.'

Roger Waters, on being (relatively) anonymous despite the group's global success, *Rolling Stone*, 19 November 1987

Lurching into the future, bearing the mantle of Pink Floyd, without Roger in 1987 was a big tough mantle to stick on my poor shoulders and trudge forward into the future with.

David Gilmour, on his reluctance to carry the band, and brand, forward into the future once Roger left, DJ Redbeard radio interview, 30 March 1994

The setlist that the reunited Pink Floyd played for Live 8, 2 July 2005.

It was the first show together as Pink Floyd with Roger Waters since 1985.

1. **"Speak to Me"**
2. **"Breathe/Breathe (reprise)"**
3. **"Money"**
4. **"Wish You Were Here"**
5. **"Comfortably Numb"**

COMFORTABLY FAMOUS

Lisbon was amusing. It was our first European gig and right from the start they had their hands over their heads, clapping time to the music, including moments when there is no time. It's very hard to keep going when you've got 80,000 people clapping to the wrong rhythm...

Rick Wright, on the group's *The Division Bell* tour, *Q* magazine, November 1994

I can't say that my greatest desire is to be innovative or break new frontiers. I just hope to make music that moves people a little bit and makes them think. We don't claim to have solutions to life's great problems.

David Gilmour, on Pink Floyd being perceived as pioneers of musical innovation, *USA Today*, 1994

COMFORTABLY FAMOUS

It's a shame we didn't manage the split better. If my children behaved like that, I'd be very cross.

Nick Mason, on the rancour caused by Roger leaving the group, *USA Today*, 1994

> It's very important to make the audience eat their meat before they can have their pudding!

Nick Mason, on the importance of only touring when there is new music to perform, *Record Collector*, March 2000

COMFORTABLY FAMOUS

> **"**
> I don't want to be in the studio making Pink Floyd records all my life. There are a lot of people in this business who are workaholics, and I'm not one of them. But I'm not quite ready for retirement. I tried it for a year, and it's harder work than working. **"**

David Gilmour, on the reason it took seven years to make *The Division Bell*, *Interview* magazine, July 1994